HOUSE PLANTS

&

How to

GROW THEM

PARKER T. BARNES

INTRODUCTION BY DYLAN RAY

MICROCOSM
PORTLAND, OR

PUBLISHING
CLEVELAND, OH

HOUSEPLANTS & HOW TO GROW THEM

© Parker T. Barnes

ISBN 9781648412585
This is Microcosm # 884
This edition © Microcosm
Publishing, 2025

For a catalog, write or visit:
Microcosm Publishing
2752 N Williams Ave.
Portland, OR 97227

All the news that's fit to print at www.Microcosm.Pub/
Newsletter.

Get more copies of this book at www.Microcosm.Pub/
Houseplants.

Get more books in this series at www.Microcosm.Pub/
HowToGrow.

MICROCOSM · PUBLISHING

MICROCOSM PUBLISHING is Portland's most diversified publishing house and distributor, with a focus on the colorful, authentic, and empowering. Our books and zines have put your power in your hands since 1996, equipping readers to make positive changes in their lives and in the world around them. Microcosm emphasizes skill-building, showing hidden histories, and fostering creativity through challenging conventional publishing wisdom with books and bookettes about DIY skills, food, bicycling, gender, self-care, and social justice. What was once a distro and record label started by Joe Biel in a drafty bedroom was determined to be *Publishers Weekly*'s fastest-growing publisher of 2022 and #3 in 2023, and is now among the oldest independent publishing houses in Portland, OR, and Cleveland, OH. Biel is also the winner of PubWest's Innovator Award in 2024. We are a politically moderate, centrist publisher in a world that has inched to the right for the past 80 years.

Publisher's Note

When we reissued *Culpeper's Complete Herbal* from 1653 in 2022, I observed how shocking it was that much of the information remains relevant nearly 400 years later. Overhearing this utterance, our Operations Manager quipped "You do believe in evolution...don't you?" starting to look a little genuinely concerned about my current brand of wingnuttery.

Plants didn't evolve so much in 400 years as changed, of course. We, on the other hand, have willfully forgotten what they can be or do in favor of the built realities of the industrial worldview. Modern humans just don't interact with nature the way we used to. My relationship with nature, for instance, has been fraught and has caused me to be rather trepidatious anytime I'm away from the confines of my porch or the sidewalk. I got poison oak on half of my body somehow at my sister's wedding. Or there was the time that I carried home a boysenberry plant on the bus and—despite my best efforts to constantly adjust it—it insisted on stabbing three passengers in the neck repeatedly.

Twenty years ago, I used to get cuts all over my body climbing down the bluffs in Portland to harvest blackberries to bake a pie. Then one day, someone decided that the city needed to burn them all down because they were an *invasive species* of blackberry. I didn't understand and attending a public hearing, I pleaded to no avail "Counterpoint: they are also edible and quite delicious." Apparently invasive species are as detested in the plant world as immigrants are in the U.S. This was largely the end of my foray of wandering into nature or making sense of the logic of how humanity interfaces with it.

Over the past 30 years, I realized that I am simply more comfortable with books about plants than I am with the plants themselves. In fact, the book that I keep next to my recliner on the deck is *Houseplants and Their Fucked Up Thoughts*, published by my pal, Angela Engel. It truly celebrates, on several levels, the pinnacle of how close I can come to being comfortable around plants. This is all much funnier because my best friend is an herbalist, constantly feeding me natural remedies from her intense knowledge and the plants that she grows in her yard.

So I read a book like this and think, "Wow, how wonderful it must be to grow plants like this in your home, have everything work out, and feel the wondrous aspects of parenthood— where you know each of them will be there when you return, growing and thriving under your care."

Just like *Culpeper's Complete Herbal*, I mostly marvel at how relevant this book is, though—to our credit—we were much quicker on the reissue this time. Speaking of the 1600s, that's when humanity realized the need to cultivate plants

indoors. Native plants grew outside for a reason—
they were naturally adapted to the local climate.
As we began to fetishize non-native plants, that's
when we started bringing them into our lives,
hence the need for sheltering them a bit, like, say,
children. Europeans developed ways to move
plants around the world in mini greenhouses
from places like East Asia, North America, and
Africa. The plants received European names,
classified according to Linneaus's taxonomy,
and were another thing that, as historian Penny
Sparke put it, humanity colonized, controlled,
and exploited. Then, when fires swept through
London, windows were re-engineered and the
windowsill was introduced in 1708, creating a
great place for all of these houseplants.

I read a book review this week where the
reporter called houseplants "mundane," which
felt both reductive and honestly kind of
insulting. And I don't even get along with plants.
Still, I know how fascinating they are. They can

be beautiful and enchanting and surprising, the ways that they cope with environments and aren't as changed by time as I'd expect. Why is my yard constantly overrun by vines, then barren for six months, followed by the roses springing six feet tall seemingly overnight? If that's mundane, sign me up for mundanity.

And then there's the whole matter of how many would-be plant parents emerged during the pandemic. Smugly, to myself, I uttered "Good luck. I know how ill-fated your cuttings are." Of course, I was entirely too smug because most of these growers were far more successful than I had ever been. In my best moments, I had been handed a successful plant and stared at it like the inexperienced, green parent that I was, terrified and waiting for it to wither before my eyes.

Seriously, though, I have the deepest regard and the mildest jealousy of people who can pull off the sort of projects in this book inside their homes. Because if this is what plants are up to, untended, like the ones in my front yard, what would transpire with a bit of nurture with that nature? I was jealous because other people were leaving me in the dirt, discovering that plants can be more than decoration.

So why are we still collecting and displaying houseplants 400 years after those windowsills displayed Londoners' infatuation with houseplants? As the population migrated from the country to density in the city, we liked the idea of keeping some greenery around. Houseplants became an area of the home where women were allowed some agency. We decided that we wanted year-round herbs and medicinal treatments, ways to cover up nasty smells, to replace clutter, a misdirection to draw the eye to where we wanted visitors looking in our homes, and cute friends to spruce up the place. We wanted to keep a plant that had lived well for a long time, take it to a hostile climate, and pamper it under its new identity. Let's not forget the aspirational American classic—keeping up with the elements of conquest—and the Joneses' plants. The truth is, most people have forgotten all of this, and just enjoy having plants around. That's a wonderful reason too. If you research any hobby too deeply, you can find things not to like about it, so it's much more important to appreciate everything that you can in life.

Anyway, why is Parker T. Barnes still relevant in the era where you can buy dozens of different books about how to decorate the interior of your home with various plants? Because he keeps it simple. Barnes wrote this book at a time that houseplants were patently uncool—before TikTok fantasies and curated AI images. He wrote it even before the resurgence of houseplants after World War 2 when—just like the pandemic—people turned inwards to think more about their homes, where they spend half of their lives. Houseplants still serve the same impetus to make spaces welcoming and nourishing. This book captures each houseplant's quirks, idiosyncrasies, and oddest behaviors. Barnes is not living out some aspirational wealth class fantasy. He wasn't flipping through fashion magazines of perfectly cultivated homes and replicating them. The dude just genuinely *liked plants*. Barnes didn't design houses to have specific places for plants. He incorporated plants into the existing design of the home. His interest is pure. And weirdly relevant today.

Maybe it's time for me to try appreciating the plants themselves again, though let's be honest. I'm quite content to take my preconceived notions, research arguments that support my knee-jerk reactions, and then argue with people, saying things like "Houseplants are fundamentally colonialist, chauvinist, classist, and problematic." And then go back to enjoying books about houseplants. We're all hypocrites—and that's okay.

The reality is that I am never going to become the plant parent with cuttings in brown water, talking about the addictive nature of begonias, stressing about whether my plants are overwatered or overgrown, lamenting my plant death toll, or debating if plants are design or decor. Still, I can recognize that plants invite onlookers to reflect on our own perceptions of the natural world and the relationships we form with them. They are beautiful and they *do* warm up the room. They remind us that there is more silently going on all around us than we often think about. Perhaps we should pay closer attention to the subtleties and complexities of the natural world—or at least enjoy more books about plants.

Introduction to the 2024 Edition

Dylan Ray, historian and 20-year plant peddler

Sulfuric acid gas from burning coal, the primary heating and power source in the Victorian Age, filled the air in cities and homes of the Industrial Era. Iron-clad plants, such as palms, ferns in terrariums, aspidistra (cast-iron plant), and many outdoor annuals gained in popularity during this period because both indoor and outdoor plants were failing due to the pollution. Initially, only the wealthy could purchase and collect these rare plants to display. The history of houseplant collecting is tied up in superiority complexes, skewed morality, and an obsession with trends and fitting in.

The Wardian case, introduced by Nathaniel Bagshaw Ward, now commonly known as a terrarium, accelerated the colonial endeavors of the British Empire by making plant clippings transportable. Tea, rubber trees, coffee, quinine, and many varieties of plant starts could be transported vast distances, which furthered the empire's efforts. Government-assigned plant collectors used this device to take a variety of plants from countries and territories from around the world and introduce them to Victorian homes. The use of interior plants to display wealth, status, and status quo morality cemented itself as a trend. Moral elitism quickly led to campaigns to use houseplants to "save the poor." Ward even titled Chapter V of his book, *On the Growth of Plants in Closely Glazed Cases*, "On the Application of the Closed Plan in improving the Condition of the Poor."

In the late-1800s US, wealthy social elites, politicians, and Progressive Era cultural leaders continued to equate morality with aesthetics according to *their* definitions of acceptable religion, design, and social norms. Fueled by Eurocentric misconceptions, they unfairly blamed urban conditions and perceived immoral behavior(s) on the working class, immigrants, people of color, and others who resided in the elite-owned, mismanaged industrial landscapes. This influenced the attempt, by the opulent and powerful, to standardize culture and make the "city beautiful" by making the poverty, living conditions, and treatment of the working class invisible.

Social and moral value again was placed on houseplants, ornamental gardens on porches, and window gardens as essential elements of the strategy to "beautify" the city. Gardening and home-improvement magazines stressed that it was the civic duty of the urban, and eventually suburban, dweller to engage with the rules of plant and garden arrangements, which was portrayed as virtuous behavior. Everything from home and yard furniture arrangements to exterior potted plants, landscaping, window gardens, and houseplants was used to signify righteousness and contributions to the social order. This created a trend that spread from the homes of the opulent to the tenements of the city dweller and many other home styles and family structures.

This is the social environment in which Parker T. Barnes published his book *Houseplants and How to Grow Them* in 1909. He had already been an active horticulturalist and author by the printing of this book. Early in life he worked at a variety of agricultural experiment stations and the St. Louis Botanical Gardens. Beginning in 1902, during the US occupation of the Philippines, Barnes spent a year in Manila as the botanical collector, classifying trees and plants for the Bureau of Forestry. He wrote articles for *Horticulture Magazine*, *The Garden Magazine*, *Suburban Life*, and a variety of newspapers. Eventually he worked for the State Department of Agriculture, the Sun Oil Company (where he worked with insecticides), and the McFarland Company, a book publisher.

Many of Barnes's articles were written for the novice homeowner or tenant and/or the practical common home. Some of these articles include "Lawn Making," "The Joys of a 'Cool Greenhouse,'" and "How to Have Berries All Summer." He explained how to use household items to create fumigators, propagating boxes, and heat-holding mechanisms. Houseplant solutions "on a budget" are a common thread throughout the writings, and he seemed to keep a focus on the layperson throughout his career. For example, Barnes held plant competitions that professionals could show at but weren't allowed to place in. The enforcement of perceived morality and ethics through the use of plants and design ultimately led to the popular literature of Barnes's time, which gave thrifty tips to working-class people with fewer traditional resources.

The houseplant-filled parlors of Victorian homes fell out of style as shifts in labor continued and new home designs became popular by necessity and trend. Houseplants became a common home feature in years after, but they were no longer such a blatant symbol of wealth or morality. There were resurgences of houseplants as integral components of modern design throughout the 1920s and again in the 1940s.

The next major surge in houseplant popularity came in the 1970s. Home and garden magazines advertised the somewhat hard lines of mid-century modern homes and designs augmented with natural elements. Another contributing factor was a rise in environmentalism as a response to the growing awareness of the pollution from industrialism. Terrariums holding ferns surged in popularity, bringing the natural environment inside, along with many of the "iron-clad" plants such as palms, spider plants, aspidistra, rubber plants, and Norfolk pines.

Trends throughout the 1980s–2000s shifted away from the abundance of plants seen in the Victorian Era and the 1970s, but never *completely* away from houseplants. A resurgence of interest started in the mid-2010s. Terrariums, succulents and cacti, common houseplants, and carnivorous plants gained consumer attention.

There are many theories as to why, including the financial effects of a "Great Recession" in 2009, such as increasing home prices, student loans for jobs that didn't arrive, and higher inflation without matching wages. This left many young consumers who would be buying homes and starting families delayed in those pursuits, renting longer, and spending more time in their homes as opposed to spending money on lavish dinners and outside expenses. Their investment in plants to caretake, trade, and curate their home environment grew the houseplant and gardening industry. Increased awareness of the effects of global climate change also brought a new green renaissance, much like in the 1970s, and the desire to engage with nature increased.

A global pandemic that started in 2020 mandated time away from people and brought many inside their homes, without work or the ability to engage with their community. This, along with the continued effects of the Great Recession and the green renaissance mentioned above, as well as revived trends from the 1970s, caused people to become involved with the caretaking of plants and increased interest in self-education texts about houseplants and gardens.

Parker T. Barnes's book lives on in this spirit, empowering everyday people with the practical knowledge they need to help their plants thrive. The text may be over 100 years old, but modern readers will find his writing and advice relevant and charmingly timeless, rather than outdated. Knowing the historical context for his work simply enriches our engagement with it, reminding us that his ultimate goal was to share with us his own profound joy in plants, regardless of our budget or social class.

PREFACE

THERE have been books on window gardens and house plants before this, and they have told, at length, of every kind of plant that under some condition or other has eked out a struggling existence in our dwellings. The purpose of the present volume is to discuss fully those plants which are *sure* to succeed. If a selection is made from the various kinds enumerated in the following pages, failure is next to impossible; it can only be brought about by carelessness and inattention to the first principles of cultivation.

Somewhat minute directions have been given for the preparation of soil, for seed sowing and for other operations in connection with each plant, and particularly as regards temperature. It should be understood that in every case these indicate the best conditions, not the imperative conditions; for success can often be achieved with wide divergence from the ideal. Still, the nearer one can attain to the proper conditions, the better and surer the results.

Although every cultural statement made is based on my own practical experience as a grower, yet the experiences of successful amateurs (as told in several numbers of the *Garden Magazine*) have been drawn upon in order to give encouragement to beginners. Particularly must I acknowledge having made extracts in Chapter I. from the writings of Mrs. M. K. Farrand, who created the piazza conservatory, and whose calendar of operations forms Chapter XVII., the cellar door conservatory was originally described by Mrs. Edith L. Fullerton; the gas stove heating arrangement was invented by Mrs. E. A. Eames, and Mr. Leonard Barron's ideas are embodied in Chapter VI. The home propagating box and the home fumigator described are original with Mr. L. J. Doogue. I also wish to thank Mr. J. D. Eisele, Mr. Peter Duff, and Mr. A. J. Manda for suggestions and assistance.

NEW YORK, 1909   P. T. B.

HOUSE PLANTS

CHAPTER I

How Other People Have Succeeded

A plain statement of facts — Practical ideas in window gardens — Glass houses for forcing in winter — Heating problems solved.

A GROUP of healthy looking, vigorous-growing house plants always fills me with delight for it must be confessed at the outset that the thoroughly successful cultivation of a large number of plants in a window garden or in any part of a dwelling house is no mean achievement. The conditions with which living plants have to contend when brought into our ordinary living rooms are trying indeed. The fluctuations of temperature are usually not only great, but also sudden; light is neither uniform nor abundant; and the atmosphere is generally excessively dry. This last condition is particularly true in the winter time, when our rooms are heated by artificial means and every degree of heat that is thus supplied for our individual comfort is taxing the energy of the plant in causing transpiration of water at a time when, normally, plant growth is at its minimum activity.

The cultivation of plants in the house, then, is very largely an individual problem of overcoming a set of opposing conditions which will never be the same for two individuals nor for the same individual in two different places. What we have to strive for is to maintain a fairly comfortable, average condition, and it is really surprising, when all things are taken into consideration, what eminently satisfactory results can be achieved. I have seen window gardens that from one year's end to another are perfect blazes of colour; in others, again, plants grown for their foliage effect alone have flourished amazingly. Yet similar plants in the homes of other people dwindled and finally died.

The ideal situation for a window garden is on the south side of the house, the window itself slightly projecting from the building line, so as to secure abundance of light, for the sunshine is the life. In addition, just because the winter and spring sun may sometimes be too energetic for plants at rest, there should be some arrangement of adjustable shades to screen the excessive light which might be injurious to some of the younger growths in the early days of spring. Plants that have been kept in dark corners of dwelling rooms — such as palms or ferns — when brought into the window garden to resuscitate, will be thankful for such careful protection while the sun is at its hottest. Many ingenious devices have been thought out by amateur gardeners to meet the requirements and to provide the necessary best available conditions for their pets, and surely if one is about to indulge in window gardening on anything like an extensive scale, it is the part of wisdom to make a good beginning by giving them the best chance possible for a comfortable life.

It is often not at all difficult to build a small extension outside a window for the accommodation of house plants, and a little addition like this, on a slightly more pretentious scale, very easily approaches the dignity of a small greenhouse; and in a great many respects will serve the same purpose, as for raising seeds of plants to be put out in the garden later, whether these be flowering plants or vegetables.

A PIAZZA CONSERVATORY

I know of one instance where a ten-foot-square corner of a piazza was brought into service by enclosing it with glass so that it might have been surely called a piazza conservatory. Its owner preferred to refer to it merely as a "glass house" on account of its small dimensions, but I venture to say that this small place gave more pleasure, and perhaps more flowers, to its owner than some other real greenhouses on a much more elaborate scale. Besides the flowers, the glass house is big enough to hold comfortably a wicker armchair and a teastand. The house is built on one corner of the porch, and gets the early morning sun from the east, and the south and west sun later in the day.

The first year a small coal stove was installed in one corner, and the temperature varied from tropical to arctic in a startling manner; but in spite of being baked one hour and chilled the next, the plants managed to survive. The coal stove was succeeded by a smokeless oil heater, which has proved, except in windy and very cold weather, a most satisfactory arrangement. The heating question was finally settled for good by running a pipe from the furnace underneath the drawing room out into the glass house.

The glass house was first furnished with some stocks and cannas taken from the garden, and some ferns and green-leaved plants. Just a few days before Christmas the first box of paper-white narcissus is in full bloom, and since then the house is not without a flower. Freesias, Chinese sacred lilies, and more paper-white narcissi follow in January, and about the middle of the month the azaleas commence and keep bravely on until the last of March. Before the flowers of the last box of narcissus wither, the early Yellow Prince tulip starts in, about the 15th of February, lasting till near the end of March.

One hundred and fifty *Gladiolus Colvillei*, planted early in January, gave dozens of white and pink flowers in the third week of May. Wistarias in large pots, and hyacinths came next, while more tulips (variety Murillo) and a huge plant of double flowering cherry (*Prunus Pseudo-Cerasus*, var. *hortensis flore-pleno*, known in the trade as *P. Sieboldii*, var. *rubra plena*) made March gay with pink tints. The calla lilies flower until May.

In such a place as this seeds of the greenhouse type of plant, such as primrose, cineraria, and calceolaria, may be started in the usual way, in flats with window glass over the boxes to prevent too rapid evaporation of the moisture, but care must be taken to secure the right soil. Finely sifted woods earth, mixed with one-third sandy loam, has proved a reliable combination in the hands of the lady who presides over the house, in which to germinate the seeds of these plants. Drainage is provided by a layer of sharp sand and bits of broken crockery and charcoal in the bottom of the box.

When the seedlings have developed three or four leaves, they are transplanted to one and one-half inch pots, using about the same soil and drainage as in the flats, adding a small quantity of well-rotted cow manure.

The pots are now plunged to the rims in sand to keep the soil moist.

As it may be of practical value to others I give, in Chapter XVII., the "calendar of operations" for this piazza house. It's valuable because it is real experience, not a table of guesses.

BUILDING ROUND A CELLAR DOOR .

Another triumphant solution of a somewhat similar problem of making a plant-house attachment to the dwelling resulted in utilizing the heat from the furnace and making a removable house around the cellar door. The story is best told by the one who did it all:

"The south door opens upon a small porch, with the outside cellar door under part of its roof. One French window also opens upon it. The floor of this porch was directly on the ground, and, as the boards had rotted away, we removed them, substituting a floor of cement.

"The cellar is low, and a modern furnace heated it beyond the point of wisdom. We sought an outlet for the heat and immediately the conservatory shaped itself. By enclosing the small porch in glass and removing the outside cellar doors, the heat from the cellar would be released and the conservatory warmed. By leaving the hall door open and removing the French windows from the living room, we gained more heat and better ventilation.

"Our desire was to have as much glass and as little wood as was possible for strength and durability. We also desired the glass panes to butt and not be puttied. It was necessary to have a door in front of the cellar door for the removal of coal ashes, and transoms for ventilation. With this general plan the work was begun. A heavy timber was run along the floor and bolted at the corners (the conservatory must disappear in summer time). A corresponding timber ran along the edge of the porch ceiling. Uprights were then placed at certain intervals, and these were grooved to admit of the glass sliding down them. Photographic plates, 11 x 14, freed from the gelatine, made the glass panes for our conservatory.

"Curtains of unbleached muslin were arranged for; the rollers, four and five feet long respectively, were of tin. These were set at the bottom, along the beam, and the curtains drawn up by means of a sash cord and pulleys.

"Two trays about table height were constructed. They were four inches deep, to admit of sand in them in which to sink the pots. A shelf was made about two inches from the floor on these tray tables, and formed an admirable place for seed boxes and for starting bulbs.

"The curtains proving insufficient protection from the sun, we coated the outside of the structure with a lime wash to keep off the direct rays. As for the heating, there was ample, and our cellar was kept in the finest condition. When the thermometer registered 4 below zero out of doors, the glass or garden room registered 56 degrees.

"The labour included cutting the glass and placing it in the frames where it was needed."

THE HEATING PROBLEM

Perhaps, after all, the greatest stumbling-block in window gardening lies in the matter of heating. Very naturally one wants to have, as the fruits of this hobby, plants in flower during the winter season. The most ingenious method I ever heard of was the construction of a miniature gas furnace in the cellar to heat a portable window extension box, and it was by no means expensive. The scheme was evolved out of the desire to force bulbs; it came as an inspiration one October day when overhauling the storm windows preparatory for winter. Two tall, narrow ones which had been made useless by remodeling the sitting-room suggested the thought that here was a start toward the little conservatory. They were of exactly the same height as the storm sash of the south dining-room window. Here, then, were three sides of a window greenhouse; moreover, they exactly fitted each other and the window.

By means of four long screws on a side,

the two narrow sashes were fastened to the window frame at the exact places where the vertical edges of the regular storm sash belonged — only they were at right angles to the wall of the house, projecting into space. The regular storm sash was now screwed to the outer edges of the two sashes already in place, forming a generous space, ideally lighted, requiring only a top and bottom to make a splendid window-conservatory.

Half-inch boards nailed across formed the bottom and two oak brackets supported the whole. Two tapering boards were fitted to the top making a roof with a pitch and overhanging eaves sufficient to shed any kind of weather. Old rubber floor matting tacked over all made the top and bottom waterproof. A tight joint with the house was made by continuing the rubber back and up under the bottom of the first clapboard.

Three six-inch shelves were placed across both side sashes by means of five-inch brackets. When still more room was necessary, additional six-inch shelves were laid across the front with their ends resting on the first set. This provided three complete tiers of shelves running around the three sides of the conservatory. Without crowding, about seventy-five pots and pans of various sizes can be accommodated here. As zero weather approached, the warmth from the dining room proved inadequate and other means of maintaining the requisite temperature to keep the plants growing were found to be necessary, so a miniature furnace was installed.

A three-eighth-inch pipe was run from the natural gas main in the cellar through the cellar window and up through the bottom of the conservatory, ending in an ordinary gas burner. This gave plenty of heat but the fumes from the gas proved objectionable and the arrangement was abandoned for the following which works admirably.

For $2.25 a tiny gas stove was purchased. This was placed on the cellar floor directly below the cellar window under the conservatory. A short smoke-pipe was connected to the nearest chimney opening in order to dispose of the fumes. A tinsmith made a galvanized iron hood which fitted down over and completely enclosed the stove; it had a number of one-inch holes along its bottom edges for circulation, and a sliding door for access to the stove. Its top was drawn up to form a collar about eight inches in diameter. From this collar an eight-inch flue ran up and out through the cellar window (from which a pane had been removed), and ended at a five by seven inch register set into the floor of the "conservatory." The flue was enclosed in a wooden box or outer flue for insulation throughout its entire length outdoors.

This formed virtually a miniature hot-air furnace. The tiniest flame warmed the stove, which in turn warmed the air enclosed in the galvanized hood. This warm air flowed up the pipe through the register and gave the plants just what they needed — pure, moist, warm air.

HEATING FROM THE LIVING ROOM

But it may not be possible always to instal a carefully designed heating plant, and many are the cases where satisfactory window gardens are maintained by the heat from the adjoining room alone — no extra apparatus — but of course no real forcing is done here. In one such simple garden, situated on the south side of the house, it is found by experience that the best results could be obtained by watering the plants frequently and keeping the adjoining library at an even temperature of 70 degrees.

About the 1st of October every year the window garden is filled with chrysanthemums, of which it holds about four dozen. These flowers last till the end of November, when they are replaced by the real winter flowers, first among which are the geraniums, which are hardy and do not require much care and will remain in flower throughout the winter. Heliotropes also do very well. Candytuft in boxes does much better than if placed singly in pots, and makes a better showing. Nasturtiums with plenty of room and strings to climb on will remain in flower all winter. Mignonette and begonias can also be grown to advantage, and do not require much care. In fact, any flower of a hardy nature will flourish in one of these gardens.

CONTROL OF TEMPERATURE

Never let the cold, frosty air strike your plants, for it will kill them; nor let the

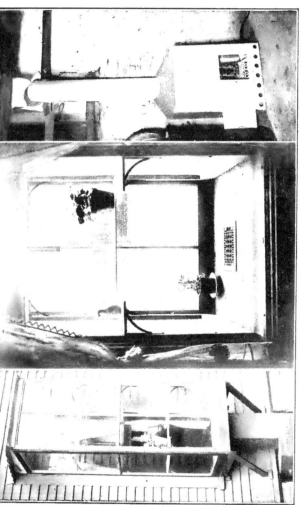

HEATING A WINDOW GARDEN

The details are given in Chapter I. By means of the miniature heater in the cellar a constant supply of warm, fresh air is delivered to the plants, which flourish all winter

AN UNHEATED WINDOW GARDEN

This collection of plants was grown entirely by the heat received from the living room, and it gave a welcome greenery all the winter

temperature of the room vary between too wide limits (20 degrees would be safe, but extreme during the day; the night temperature can be as much as 10 degrees below the day minimum). If at one time the plants are overheated, and the next moment chilled, their growth is stunted and their bloom killed.

CHAPTER II

MAKING THE SOIL FOUNDATION

The ideal and practical substitutes — Loam and when to get it — The compost heap — Spring *vs.* fall making — Manures of various kinds — Leafmould —Peat — Muck.

GOOD soil is an absolute necessity to success with plants and there is only one way to get it — by mixing. A workable soil may be made from loam, sand, and manure, but it will be much better if it has an addition of leafmould, peat, or well-weathered muck.

When it is impracticable to make a compost heap, any good garden loam may be used and it is not absolutely necessary to prepare it any length of time beforehand.

PASTURE LOAM FOR COMPOST

The best loam to use in a potting soil is well decayed sod taken from a pasture. The best time to secure it is in the fall after the grass has been killed by hard frosts; it can, however, be secured in the spring before the grass starts to grow. Cut the sod three or four inches deep and place it in a pile, the grass side down. For convenience make the pile about four feet wide and high, and as long as necessary, and have the top hollowed out a little so that it will catch the rains and so keep the pile moist. Many people when making up the sod pile compost manure with it. If you prefer to do it this way add one part fresh cow manure to each three parts of sod, if done in the fall.

ADDING MANURE

When the compost is made in the spring the manure must be well-rotted, and horse manure is preferable to cow manure.

The compost pile must be thoroughly mixed two or three times by chopping it down with a spade and throwing it up into a new pile.

A spring-made compost heap will be ready to use in the fall, but the soil is apt to be rather coarse. The fall-made compost is sure to give much better satisfaction.

In my practice I have always found well-decayed horse manure better than cow manure; the latter can be used, however, but it tends to make the soil cold and clammy. Well-decayed horse manure may usually be purchased in the suburbs and smaller towns from the livery or other stables. If you cannot purchase rotted horse manure and you have a convenient place in any out-of-the-way corner in the backyard where fresh droppings can be stored, well and good. They will require several months to rot properly. Protect it from the rain and turn it over frequently to prevent burning. If the manure gets too dry sprinkle it with water when turning.

Sheep, hen, pigeon, and other manures may be used in mixing potting soils, but very sparingly, for they are so strong that if a large amount is used the roots of the plants will be burned.

LEAFMOULD, PEAT, AND MUCK

Added to the potting soil, either leafmould, peat or muck makes it much more friable, increases its water-holding capacity, eases the circulation of the air through it, and induces a better growth of roots. In no case is there actual fertilizing value. In raising from seed such plants as cyclamens, cinerarias, Chinese primroses and begonias, leafmould is a necessity. Where manure is not obtainable one of these three forms of vegetable mould must be used to supply the necessary humus; the plant food can then be added in the form of a complete fertilizer which may be bought from any seedsman.

Peat is very scarce in this country, and so is quite expensive; but it can be bought from nearly all the dealers in seeds or bulbs.

Leafmould and muck are much easier to obtain, and usually cost nothing outside of the labour necessary to collect them. When the foliage is falling, late in September or in October, is the best time to lay in a stock of next year's leafmould.

If there is no hardwood timber land nearby, where you can get clean leaves, then rake up the leaves which have fallen in the street. Maple leaves are best, but those of the elm and oak will do. Sometimes an arrangement can be made with the city employees to dump in the back yard all the leaves they gather in cleaning the streets. In this way, and at no cost, an abundant supply of leafmould can be had in suburban districts.

HANDLING LEAVES

In the winter the leaves may be used for banking coldframes and pits, to keep out the frost, or for mulching the bulb beds. In the spring, when the pits are empty, throw all the leaves into a pit, wet them thoroughly, and allow them to rot. By fall they are in good condition to use. If this way of rotting them is followed, you will probably need to wet them several times during the summer. Another good way to handle the leaves is to dig as large a hole in the ground as you can fill with leaves. Pack in the leaves as tightly as possible, wetting them as they are being . thrown in. A good time to do this is on a rainy day, for then it saves the necessity of handling water. If you have a hose you can do the work at any time.

If neither of these ways can be followed, the leaves may be put in a heap on the ground, thoroughly moistened, and tramped down. When treated thus, it will be necessary to water them oftener, because the pile presents more surface from which the moisture can evaporate. Turn the heap of leaves occasionally, and in two years the leaf-mould will be in usable condition.

Never bury leaves in your garden where you intend to grow plants next year. The heat caused by the fermentation will injure the roots of the growing plants.

VALUE OF MUCK

Muck from either a fresh water or salt water marsh is equally good as leafmould, but it must be dug at least one winter before using. After digging, place it on the upland, away from the tides and floods, in triangular-shaped piles about three feet wide, three feet high, and as long as necessary. By putting it in such small piles the frost and air have a much better chance to work through it than if it is in larger piles. Under ordinary circumstances, exposure to the weather for one winter will sweeten it. But if not, add a little lime; this will quickly neutralize any acidity.

DRAINAGE

One of the most important things to provide for in a soil is drainage. This is best secured by adding sand. Use a clean, sharp sand such as a mason would use for making mortar. If you cannot secure this from a nearby sand bank, you can buy bird sand, if only small quantities are needed, from the grocer. It comes put up in small packages. If sand from the seashore is used, get it from the shore side of the sand hills, and wash it thoroughly before using in order to remove any salt. Although I have never done it myself, I have seen coal ashes successfully used as a substitute for sand. They were, of course, screened to remove the coarse matter. On heavy soils coal ashes sometimes are a positive detriment, however, by making the clay into a sort of cement. Where better drainage is wanted than can be given by simply adding sand, add charcoal. If the plants are to stay for a year or so in single pots without repotting (as is the case with palms), the charcoal is a distinct advantage, not only because of the better drainage it affords, but also because it prevents the soil from souring. Charcoal is cheap, and a little of it goes a long way.

It is very important to have on hand

at all times the ingredients necessary to make up a good potting soil, so in an outbuilding away from the weather, or in the cellar, have bins in which a six months' (if not a year's) supply, of the articles just mentioned may be stored. You will find this a very decided advantage, especially in the winter when the ground is frozen. Even the manure may be stored in the cellar, if it is well decayed, without the least inconvenience.

No hard and fast rule can be laid down for the amounts of the different ingredients of a potting soil. They will vary with the character of the soil in your locality. I have found that a soil composed of equal parts of rotted sod, manure, leafmould, and sand will give excellent results with plants ordinarily grown in the house. If the rotted sod has been composted then it will be necessary to add only sand and leafmould.

Mix the soil thoroughly before planting. The best way to do this is to get the component parts together in layers, and then throwing the mass over to making a new pile. Always shovel from the bottom of the pile, and always throw the added matter on the apex of the new pile so that the soil can roll down the sides. If this is done, and the pile turned three or four times, the soil will be thoroughly mixed.

Before mixing the soil determine whether it is sufficiently moist. This may be told by taking a handful of the soil and pressing it firmly in the hand. If water can be squeezed out the soil is too damp, and ought not to be worked over until enough dry soil has been added to take up the surplus moisture.

If, after having been pressed in the hand, the soil remains together, but will break upon being lightly touched, it contains the proper amount of moisture. If it will not remain in a lump but breaks up immediately the pressure is released, it needs more water. Add it by means of a watering pot; the amount necessary can be judged better from experience than by any rules which may be laid down.

CHAPTER III

Potting and Repotting

When to repot — Why plants die — Feeding vs. shifting — Winter disturbance — "Knocking out" — Seedlings — Cuttings — The potting bench — Crocking and drainage — Danger of large pots.

THE best time of the year to repot house plants is in the spring (April or May), or when new growths start. Only in very exceptional cases do house plants need repotting during the winter; this is particularly true of palms, ferns, rubber plants, etc. These plants are then resting or are making very little growth, and meddling is positively dangerous to their lives. The average amateur gardener does not realize this, and, although the plant is in a good, healthy condition, he becomes very much worried because it is not making new growth. Then he will repot the plant, putting it in a larger pot, and nine times out of ten the plant becomes sickly and often dies in a few weeks because of the shock received and the inability to make a new root system rapidly, and so take hold of the new soil.

FEEDING *vs.* REPOTTING

Soft-wooded plants, like geraniums and coleus, I would much rather feed with liquid fertilizer than repot during the winter; although, if the plants are growing, they may be shifted to slightly larger pots without injury. Should you desire to repot the plants, do so before the roots circling about the inside of the pot become woody; after they have matted but while still white and succulent.

HOW TO "KNOCK OUT"

To remove the plant from its pot, take the pot in the right hand and place the stem of the plant between the index and middle fingers of the left hand; then invert it and strike the edge of the pot sharply against the edge of the bench. The ball of earth and roots will slide out easily, unless the earth is dry; in that case, before attempting to remove the plant, immerse it in water until the earth has become damp.

Now, with the right hand, disentangle and

spread out the lower half of the mass of roots. If part of the ball of earth crumbles away, it does not matter. Then place enough soil in the new pot to bring the plant in about the right position — that is, with the surface (which should be loosened up) of the old ball about half an inch to one inch, according to size, below the rim of the pot.

The potting stick (see page 58) will be useful in firming the soil.

When removing palms, rubber plants, and other comparatively large-rooted plants from the pots, the roots will be found matted together in circles. If possible, without injuring the roots, remove the old drainage. This will leave a large hole in the ball. Before putting the plant in the new pot, fill up this hole with soil; otherwise it will allow the water to drain away too rapidly, and the interior of the ball becomes too dry. Sometimes the roots are so matted that it is impossible to remove the drainage.

POTTING UP CUTTINGS AND SMALL PLANTS

Cuttings and seedlings are usually first potted up in thumb pots (two-inch), from which they are shifted to larger pots as soon as the pots have become filled with roots. The soil used in filling these small pots must be free from all lumps. The better way to pot these small plants is to hold the cutting with the left hand and with the right hand fill in the soil. When the pot is full, firm the soil with the thumbs and then give the pot a sharp rap on the bench to settle the soil.

Another way to pot up cuttings (but which I believe is not so good as the way already described, because the roots are much more liable to get bunched together) is to fill the pots with soil and then make a hole in the soil for the roots, after which the soil is firmed. This is also a slower method.

LIFTING IN LATE FALL

When potting plants in the fall which have been outdoors in the flower beds all summer, select only stocky, healthy plants.

Dig them carefully so as to secure as many roots as possible. If the soil is clayey, it must be neither so wet that it is muddy and the roots cling together, nor so dry that the dirt crumbles entirely away from them. The right condition of soil can be obtained by a thorough watering at least five hours before potting.

If the plants are growing in sandy soil, it is better to have it rather dry, for then more of the working roots can be saved than if it is wet.

After potting thoroughly water the plants and set them in a shaded place. Syringe the foliage several times a day until the roots have taken hold of the new soil; but under ordinary conditions, the soil will not again need watering until the new roots have been made. As soon as the plants have taken hold, gradually inure them to direct sunlight.

MAKING WORK EASY

Potting is done best on a bench which is about waist high. For the window garden a portable affair will be found the most satisfactory. An old kitchen table on three sides of which some boards, about a foot wide, have been fastened to keep the soil from failing upon the floor will serve the purpose.

The best way to work the soil in among the roots is to hold the plant with the left hand, put a little soil around the roots, and work the plant up and down a little. Put in some more soil, and tamp it down with a potting stick. It is possible to get the soil too firm, so use the potting stick with moderation, and be careful not to strike the roots.

A potting stick is usually made from a piece of pine about a foot long, an inch wide, and an inch thick, with the corners and ends rounded off. A piece of a broom handle is sometimes used.

If the soil contains many lumps or coarse pieces of sod (as sometimes happens when the sod is not completely rotted), screen them out before potting. This will be necessary if the pots are small — six-inch and smaller — with larger pots it will make but little difference. The ordinary ash sieve is just the thing for this. Or you can make a sieve from a small box, say about eighteen inches square, cut off at a depth of three inches, and the bottom covered in with wire screen netting which has a quarter-inch or three-eighth-inch mesh, and sift the dirt through this. Save the coarse material, it will be useful when potting.

In the bottom of each pot put some coarse drainage. Broken pots are usually used for this, but coal clinkers or stones are just as good. Use whichever is the handiest. Broken charcoal is very good also. The larger sizes of pots — three-inch and up — need crocking; use from a quarter of an inch to two inches of drainage according to the size of the pot. If you use broken pots, put the pieces in with the convex side up; the crocks will fit better. Over this drainage put some of the coarse screenings to keep the finer soil from washing down through. If there are no coarse screenings, use sphagnum moss.

THE FALLACY OF LARGE POTS

Don't work on the principle that the larger the pot and the more soil, the thriftier the plant. It is not the amount of food available, but the amount assimilated, that counts. As a rule, any pot which seems to be in proportion to the plant, holding soil enough to keep it from being top-heavy, will be sufficiently large. Most amateurs make a mistake in the size of the pot, using one a size or two too large. It is very easy, indeed, to over-pot a plant, strange as it may seem, and really nothing in the plant's life can be more disastrous than an overlarge pot. Nine times out of ten the plants will be over-watered and the soil become sour.

Pots may be obtained at almost any hardware store. Buy the heavier ones, as the very thin ones now manufactured by some firms dry out too quickly. Soak new pots in water until they get through "bubbling"; otherwise, the soil of the newly potted plants will dry out too quickly. If the pots are old and green with algæ, clean them by scrubbing them with sand and water, for the "green" makes them less porous, and old earth dried on the inside surface interferes with the new root-growth.

If potting is to be done with soil which has been mixed for some time, determine by the method described in the previous chapter whether or not it has sufficient moisture. If it has not, spread the soil out thinly on the bench, water it, and then turn it a couple of times to evenly distribute the moisture as directed on page 52.

CHAPTER IV

Raising Plants from Seeds

The seed soil — Flats *vs.* pots — Sowing the seeds —
Depth to cover — Watering — Pricking out the
young plants — Transplanting — Possibilities of the
window garden — Most easily grown plants.

Many of the best house plants can be
raised from seed in the ordinary living
rooms, or where potted plants are grown
in a window during winter. It is a question
whether you actually save anything by
raising your own plants; in all probability
you could get them as cheaply and as good,
if not better, from the florist, but there is
no question about the fun in growing plants
from the seed. There is a satisfaction in
having things all your own, and the work
offers engagement indoors at a time when
gardening work outdoors is slack.

HOME MADE "FLATS"

Where only a few plants are to be started,
unglazed pots or seed-pans are often used,

but "flats" are cheaper. To make these buy from a grocery store some soap boxes. A convenient size is twelve by fifteen inches. Cut them into three-inch sections and nail bottoms on these, taking care to leave cracks between the boards or make four or five one-inch holes for drainage. The sides may be painted, if they are to be used in the house. These flats are better than pots both for starting the seed and pricking off, as they save care in watering, room, time, and trouble and the moisture in the soil is much more constant than in a small pot.

The flats being ready mix the soil. A good seed soil is made from equal parts (1) fibrous loam from the compost heap, (2) sand, and (3) leafmould, woods earth, or peat.

Over the holes or cracks in the flats put a one-half-inch layer of broken potsherds, coal clinkers, or gravel for drainage. Then put through a sieve part of the already mixed seed soil. You will then have two lots of soil, one coarse the other fine. Spread a one-half-inch layer of the coarse material over the drainage material that is already in the flat and on top of that fill the flat to within half an inch of the top with the fine, screened soil. Pack the soil in the corners and along the edges with your hands, because if you do not, it will settle there more than in the middle, and the waterings will wash down the soil, uncovering and often taking the seed with it. Firm the whole by means of a damp brick or board.

SOWING THE SEED

Make drills about two inches apart using a piece of narrow board as a marker, merely pressing it lightly into the soil for a quarter-inch or so. Sow the seeds thinly and evenly in the drills, and cover lightly; the best way to cover the seeds is to screen the soil on them, using a screen which has a mesh about the size of that in mosquito netting. A good rule to follow when covering seeds is to put on a layer of soil which is as deep as the diameter of the seeds. Sand, dry sphagnum, cocoanut fibre, or leafmould which has been rubbed through a fine screen, make very good coverings for seeds. They never get hard or bake, making an ideal covering — light, easily pushed through by the tender seed-shoots, and retentive of moisture.

Water the soil thoroughly after sowing. The best way is to set the flat in a large pan partly filled with water, allowing it to soak up from below. This is better than overhead watering because no matter how fine a spray is used it is liable to wash the soil. Another way is to water through a sheet of blotting paper. Place the blotting paper on top of the seed bed and slowly apply the water, allowing it to soak through the paper. The drip is thus avoided.

Cover the box with a loose-fitting pane of glass to keep a more humid atmosphere, thus reducing evaporation from the soil. Every day remove the glass and wipe off any water of condensation which may be on it. Place the flat in a position where it will receive all the light possible, but shade it from the direct sunlight.

THE DETAIL OF "PRICKING OUT"

Pricking out is the first transplanting of the seedlings, and needs to be done tenderly. As a rule as soon as the seedlings have made their first two real leaves it is time to "prick out" into other flats, prepared similarly to the seed flat.

Do not try to take each single seedling from the seedbed. Take out a portion of soil which has a number of seedlings in it, lay it on its side and gently separate the soil.

The dibble is a very useful tool for this purpose. It is made from a small piece of wood one-fourth or three-eighths of an inch square, or round, and about four inches long. Make a tapering point — two inches long — on one end; the other should be drawn down to an edge. This latter will be very useful in separating the plants and firming the soil about the seedling when it has been set in the new soil.

Put the little plants in rows an inch or two apart, water thoroughly, and shade for several days from hot sun with newspapers. Do not water again until the surface of the soil begins to dry. Do not delay the pricking off, do it just as soon as the little seedlings can be handled, for they may all be lost by "damping off," or they may become drawn. Should the seedlings begin to damp off apply some hot sand, sprinkling it on with a fine-meshed sieve.

As soon as the plants need still more room prick them out singly into thumb (two-inch) pots. When transplanting insert the plantlet a little deeper than it was in the old bed.

THE FATAL FROST

All the plants named later in this chapter can be grown in an ordinary window, where ordinary living room conditions prevail. The temperature should be from 50 degrees to 55 degrees at night, and under no circumstances must the freezing point be reached. The day temperature, if you can control it, may be allowed to rise 10 degrees on dull days and 15 degrees or 20 degrees will do no harm when the sun shines.

RED BERRIES FOR CHRISTMAS

Nothing is easier for the owner of a sunny window than to grow a few plants of the Jerusalem cherry (*Solanum Pseudo-Capsicum*), as the spare room is needed only when the weather gets warm outside. I don't know of a more generally satisfactory Christmas plant either. It is symmetrical, full of bright red berries, and may easily be had with a head a foot in diameter for the holidays from seeds sown during winter or spring. The "cherries" hang on for three months but in a gas laden atmosphere the leaves soon drop off.

Sow the seeds in February, and as the plants fill their pots with roots, shift to a slightly larger pot.

During summer, plunge them in a partially shady place outdoors, and give plenty of water. By pinching back, and turning, the plants may be kept symmetrical. When taken into the house in the fall, see that they get plenty of air and plenty of water at the roots, and syringe the foliage. Be careful about watering while the fruit is setting and ripening. To carry the plants over from one year to the next, cut back the old plants in the spring, and give the same treatment as they had the previous summer.

A PLANT FOR BASKETS

The best decorative plant for shelves, baskets, or hanging baskets is the foliage asparagus (*A. Sprengeri*). Its foliage is much coarser than that of the fine-leaved asparagus (*A. plumosus*), somewhat resembling light, glossy-green pine-needles, stuck endwise upon viney stems. But its branches hang down gracefully on all sides, and make a handsome, symmetrical plant. If kept growing freely all summer the plant will produce an abundance of red berries about Christmas time, making a welcome addition at that season.

VINES THAT FLOWER ALL WINTER

I think no plants are more artistic, more beautiful for room decoration than the climbing vines. The fact that they are so seldom used for this purpose gives them an added distinction. For myself, I prefer the ivies, on account of their simple strength and grace; and they are best got at the florist's. But several good house vines are best raised from seed. The cup-and-saucer-flower (*Cobæa scandens*), and *Thunbergia alata*, with its varieties, are the best two flowering vines for the house. The former has purple, bell-shaped flowers, two inches across, the latter having, according to the variety, blooms of golden yellow, rich orange, white and blue, or pure white, with white or dark centres, and about one and one-half inches across. Both these plants are perennials, but are often grown as annuals. They are easily raised from seed, are strong, rapid growers, and have very decorative foliage.

If seeds are sown early in the year — January or February — the plants can be used outdoors during the summer, and in September may be cut back, dug up, and potted for the window garden. By making successive sowings once a month until the end of May, the Thunbergia may be had in bloom all winter. The Cobœa seeds must always be set edgewise in the ground.

Two other vines which will give lots of pleasure if you have a sunny window are nasturtiums and morning-glory. I have seen morning-glory make a growth of six or seven feet when grown in an ordinary cigar box. The flowers and foliage were not as large as they would have been if grown out-doors, still the plants were healthy and flowered freely, affording much pleasure to the grower.

The nasturtium will produce a wealth of red and yellow flowers, but it absolutely demands an abundance of sunlight; if you cannot grow it in a south window where it will receive direct rays from the sun for the greater part of the day, flowers need not be expected. Seeds sown in July or August in two-inch pots, from which they are shifted to four-inch, and later to six-inch pots, will flower some time about Thanksgiving or Christmas, and will continue flowering the rest of the winter. A six-inch pot is sufficiently large for one plant, but very pretty effects can be made by growing six or seven plants in a larger pot, say nine- or ten-inch and training them over a trellis.

VINES GROWN FOR FOLIAGE

The smilax of the florists (*Asparagus medeoloides*, also known as *Myrsiphyllum asparagoides*) is also one of the best vines for the amateur's window garden. Planted in boxes, it can be trained to the window cases. The shaded places in the window garden are admirably adapted to its necessities, so it can be used where other green plants refuse to grow. The plant will make a growth ten feet long, and must have a string to climb upon. The foliage is a dark, glossy green, and there are single white flowers in winter, which are very fragrant. The seeds must be sown in January or February, and when the young plants are two or three inches high, and are making their characteristic leaves, transplant them singly to two-inch pots. In May they will need shifting to three-inch pots.

July is the time when the florists plant them out in beds in the greenhouse, but in the window garden, where a bed is not possible, I use a long, narrow box, six inches wide, as much deep, and two feet long. In this five plants are set. This is a little closer than the florists plant them, but as I have only a single row, it gives them plenty of room for development. The soil should be very rich — a fibrous loam, to which is added half-rotted cow manure and sand, one part each to three parts of loam.

The strings must be arranged just as soon as the seedlings are planted. The best material for this, because of its strength and colour, is the green smilax string used by florists, from whom it may be bought. Should you desire to use the smilax for festooning elsewhere about the house, the strings with the twining vine may be cut, and the roots will immediately start a new growth of stem. Make a new sowing of seed each year, as it does not pay to hold the plants over from one year to another. They need a night temperature of 50 degrees to 65 degrees.

ASPARAGUS THIRTY FEET HIGH

The most popular of the so-called asparagus ferns, *A. plumosus*, var. *nanus*, may be trained in vine form, too. I have seen this "dwarf" growing to the height of thirty or forty feet, with great stems like tangled creepers in a jungle. This is the best variety, because it can be used for short sprays, as a decorative pot plant, or as a vine. There is no foliage more beautiful than the delicate, light green, feathery sprays of this asparagus, and yet, in spite of its fairy-lace appearance, when cut it keeps both its colour and freshness for a very long time.

This plant is a slow grower, and it is important to have fresh seed. Sow in a good, light seed soil — *i. e.*, one having plenty of leafmould and sand in it. When the young plants begin to make good root growth, transplant to three or four inch pots. This size pot will be sufficiently large for the plants all next winter. If the growth is too long and straggly, pinch back, as is necessary. In the summer time you must decide how you wish to grow the plants — as dwarfs, or as vines.

To grow a handsome pot plant which can be used for decoration anywhere in the house, shift the young plants to a five or six inch pot, and use a good, rich, but well-drained soil. When the new growths are a foot or so long pinch out the ends. This will keep the plant dwarfed and shapely.

To grow as a vine, plant in boxes just like smilax, and be very particular that the soil and boxes are well drained.

The seeds of this asparagus are expensive, because it does not fruit freely.

IN FLOWER ALL THE YEAR

Of course you will want flowers, as well as green foliage. Perhaps the very best all-purpose flowering plant is *Primula obconica*, var. *grandiflora*, which is not tender, and blooms the whole twelve months. It is the most graceful of all primroses. Its large, single flowers are borne in clusters on the tops of stems which are four to ten inches high, and their pale, white cheeks just tinged with blue or blushed with rose. In well-grown specimens the individual flowers are often an inch and a half across. The leaves are almost round, sometimes four inches in diameter, borne on long stems, and forming a rosette supporting the flower stalks. The hairs on the leaves are irritating or poisonous to some people, which accounts to some extent for the plant not being more popular. Certainly it will grow in a more varied range of temperature, and flower longer than any other house plant.

Sow the seed any time from January to March. It may be sown later, but unless you have a coldframe in which to shade the seedlings, the young plants will be more difficult to manage. By May the seedlings should be ready for thumb-pots. A few days after potting, give abundance of air — though keep shaded — and never allow them to get dry. Syringe them on bright mornings, and after the middle of September keep the temperature about 50 degrees at night. In potting and repotting — they will require several shifts — take care not to press in too firmly about the roots, and not to cover the crowns of the plants.

The one plant which will give the greatest amount of satisfaction on more distinct counts than any other in the window is the cherry pie (*Heliotropium Peruvianum*). The beautiful purple colour of the flowers combined with the sweet, spicy perfume (whence its English name) and the long period of bloom, combine to make this an ideal window garden plant.

Originally the heliotrope flowers were violet coloured and borne in trusses about two inches across, but now, after much improvement by breeding, they are also to be found in several shades of purple and even white, and the individual trusses six inches across.

Grown in pots or boxes, a plant will ultimately cover a space about eighteen inches square, and attain a height of a foot or fifteen inches.

If you want to do something a little unusual, grow a few of the plants to a tree form. When handled this way four crops of flowers can be had from one plant from May to October. Such plants are extremely useful for hall and porch decoration.

Sow the seeds at any time from February to May, and grow the plants in pots all summer, as the heliotrope objects to removal or any interference with its roots.

If the plants are kept in the dwelling house during the summer, give as cool and moist an atmosphere as possible, for though they like sunlight, too much dry heat will scorch both leaves and flowers. Pinch back the plants wanted for winter flowers so as to give them a stocky form and to prevent them from making flowers in the summer. If possible, plunge them outside in the flower border, turning them once in a while to prevent their rooting through the hole in the bottom of the pot. Take them into the house upon the approach of cold weather. Plunging means setting the potted plant in the soil, up to the rim of the pot. This keeps the roots cool.

SUCCESS WITH MIGNONETTE

Measured by the fragrance alone I believe that the mignonette (*Reseda odorata*) is by far the best window plant for home raising. The pyramidal flower heads are unattractive in colour, but they exhale a most delicious odour — there is nothing else just like it.

Mignonette is very hard to transplant; indeed it is impossible to do it without giving the plants a check, and the secret of growing good mignonette lies in growing it on without a check at any stage of its growth. For winter bloom sow the seeds in July, August, or September. July-sown seed will bloom in November. Instead of sowing in flats sow directly in pots.

Prepare as described for flats as many two-inch pots as you wish plants to grow. Make a slight depression in the soil in the centre of each and drop into it two or three seeds, covering lightly with soil. When the seed has germinated (about two weeks) thin to one plant to a pot, retaining the strongest. When the pot has become filled with roots shift to four-inch pots and as soon as these are full of roots shift to eight-inch pots. When giving this last shift put in a two-inch layer of drainage. Be very careful not to over-water or the soil will sour; but, on the other hand, mignonette must never get dry

— that would cause a check. For the same reason never allow the plants to become pot-bound.

When the plants get about four inches high, pinch out the centre of the middle shoot. Two or three new shoots will come out from the stem, and these, with the five or six which have developed, will make a well-shaped plant. Pinch out any other shoots which may start. When the plants get about six inches high, they will need staking. For this, use small, round stakes that will be inconspicuous — birch or willow twigs are excellent for this — putting one to each stem.

When the plants get about ten inches high, and before the flower heads show, pinch out the tops of the stems so as to induce all the shoots to flower at the same time. When the flower buds commence to show, give the plants weak manure water for about a week, if the pots are well filled with roots. As the buds develop, give it oftener — say about twice a week. If you have grown the mignonette carefully without a check, there is no reason why you should not have nice plants, bearing anywhere from a dozen to fifteen good spikes. The mignonette is a cool-loving plant, and it is said that plants grown in a cool temperature will produce more fragrant flowers than those grown in a warm temperature.

I have never grown, nor have I seen, snapdragon (*Antirrhinum majus*) in the house, but I would not hesitate to try it. In a cool greenhouse it is almost as easy to grow as weeds. It can be had in beautiful spikes a foot long, and in white, yellow, and red.

For flowers the following winter, sow the seed in July, or early in August, and grow on the plants as rapidly as possible, shifting them from the two inch pots in which they are started to four inch, and, later, five or six inch, when they demand it.

THE LOVELY CYCLAMEN

No plant gives better satisfaction than the Persian cyclamen (*C. latifolium*). It is well worth trying in the window garden. Its flowers last a long time in good condition, and it has a wealth of colour. The flowers are very curiously shaped, reminding one of its relative the shooting star (Dodecatheon).

They are white or varying in different shades of pink to very dark rose colour, with a purple blotch at the mouth. There is a form the petals of which have fringed edges.

These are best grown from seed, and so constant are some of the strains that one can buy named forms which come true. The largest flowered form is called giganteum, but the large flowers are produced at the expense of quantity, so the amateur would better content himself with the good strain of a smaller flowered form. It takes fifteen months to grow the cyclamens from seed to flower, and they must never receive a check. When through flowering throw the bulbs away; they do not do well when held over.

For spring flowers the seeds are sown in November or December. These are slow to appear above ground because a little bulb is formed before the first leaf shows. As soon as two leaves have been made, transplant the seedlings to four or five inch pots, placing several in a pot, and putting them near the outside. These young seedlings are very apt to suffer from too much water and over-potting — when the plants have about half a dozen leaves shift them to three inch pots. They will not need another shift until the middle of summer when I should put them into four inch pots. In September shift them to five or six inch pots, in which they will flower. The best soil is a good fibrous loam and leafmould, well-decayed horse manure, and sand in about equal parts.

Directions for raising cactus, etc., are given in my pamphlet *Succulents and How to Grow Them.* (www.Microcosm.Pub/HowToGrow.)

Other plants which may be grown from seed successfully in the house are:

Flowering maple, *Abutilon striatum;* Floss flower, *Ageratum Mexicanum;* Amethyst, *Browallia demissa (elata);* Chimney bell flower, *Campanula pyramidalis;* Cigar plant, *Cuphea platycentra;* Trumpet flower, *Datura cornucopia;* Dragon plant, *Dracæna indivisa;* Balsam, *Impatiens Balsamina;* Cypress vine, *Ipomœa Quamoclit;* Mina, *Ipomœa versicolor (Mina lobata);* Lemon verbena, *Lippia citriodora;* Ice plant, *Mesembryanthemum crystallinum;* Wax plant, *Mesembryanthemum tricolor.* Another wax plant, *Hoya carnosa*, is propagated by division or by cuttings. Fig marigold,

Mesembryanthemum cordifolium, var. *varie-gatum;* Musk plant, *Mimulus moschatus;* Flowering tobacco, *Nicotiana affinis; Nicotiana sylvestris, Nicotiana Sanderæ;* Oxlip, *Primula elatior;* Chinese primrose, *Primula Sinensis;* Baby primrose, *Primula Forbesi;* Scarlet sage, *Salvia splendens;* Wishbone plant, *Torenia Fournieri;* Canary-bird vine, *Tropæolum Canariense;* Madagascar periwinkle, *Vinca rosea;* White periwinkle, *Vinca rosea*, var. *alba;* Pansy, *Viola tricolor.*

CHAPTER V

PROPAGATION BY CUTTINGS, ETC.

The sand bed — Temperature — A home-made propagating box — Making a cutting — Propagating
from leaves, roots, and offsets — Geraniums —
Dracænas — Umbrella plant — Making new rubber
plants.

IT is easy, indeed, to grow from seeds
such plants as are described in the preceding
chapter; but this is impossible with the
named varieties of fuchsias, geraniums,
and such like. Then, again, seeds of
such things as rubber plant and screw
pine are seldom offered for sale. There-
fore, one must resort to some other means
of propagation.

Cuttings or slips, made from pieces of
the stem or root or leaf, are generally
used. Sometimes, however, increase is by
some form of division of the roots; each
plant has its own particular method. But
most of the plants which may be grown
easily in the house, and which are not

grown from seed, may be grown from cuttings of the stem.

THE SAND BED

The best medium in which to root cuttings is damp sand. An ordinary soap box, cut down so as to be about six inches deep, will furnish sufficient space to root all the cuttings necessary to supply any ordinary window garden. In the bottom bore five or six one-inch holes, and put a layer about an inch deep of broken pots, gravel, or broken up coal clinkers for drainage. Over this put a little sphagnum moss to keep the sand from sifting down through the drainage; then put in a three or four inch layer of sand; moisten and pack it down with a brick. Have it perfectly level. The bed is now ready for the cuttings.

One drawback to the home propagation of plants is the great fluctuation of temperature. If enough bottom heat can be given so that the temperature of the sand can be kept about 80 degrees day and night and the box deep enough so that a piece of glass or newspaper can be placed over the top without injuring the cuttings, the difficulty can be got around.

HOME-MADE PROPAGATING BOX

One amateur solved the problem in a very simple and inexpensive way. This is how he did it:

"Three boxes are necessary. Soap boxes will do, if the length and width are equal, so that they will closely fit upon one another. Besides these, there will be needed a large, deep pan; two half-gallon jugs; sufficient zinc to serve as a bottom for one of the boxes; one peck of coarse sand, and a foot heater, such as is used in carriages during the winter.

"Using one of the boxes as a base, bore a few holes near the top for ventilators, which can be controlled by the use of corks. In this lower box place jugs filled with hot water during the day, when little heat will be required. At night use the foot heater, putting in about one-half cake of fuel just before retiring. Take off the top of one of the boxes and nail strips along the sides wide enough to hold the pan of water. This box will rest over the compartment with the heater. Cut the last box so that the back is about three inches higher than the front, in order to get the best distribution of light. Fill it to the depth of three inches with coarse sand.

"This is the upper box, and should be covered with a pane of glass. If these boxes fit tightly upon one another so no heat can escape, and if the jugs and pan are filled with hot water, a temperature of 80 degrees can be maintained all day by filling the jugs two or three times. Keep a small thermometer plunged in the sand, and for a few days before putting in your cuttings experiment to ascertain under just what conditions the heater will do the most satisfactory work.

"I filled the box with cuttings from rubber plants, plunging them in the sand without other preparation than cutting them with a sharp knife, leaving the surface clean and smooth. I did not lose one of the lot. Rubber plants grow so tall after a few years that one feels impelled to shorten them. This can easily be accomplished by cutting off the top and rooting it. Young plants may also be started from each joint of the old stem, thus from one old plant which has outgrown its usefulness a great many can be raised easily. After the rubber plants I put in *Pandanus Veitchii* with success. Then I took a few large leaves of *Begonia Rex*, cut the ribs on the back, made a number of incisions in the leaves, and then placed them on the sand, pressing them down to make a good contact all around. ·From each incision a plant started, and in six weeks I potted off twenty-five sturdy, clean begonias from five leaves.

"During the day I kept my bed in a good light near the window, ventilated it by raising the glass, protected it with paper when the sun was strong, and at night, when cold, I threw a carriage robe over it. From the results I have had I feel convinced that the little propagating bed is as practical as the larger ones used in greenhouses, and will do the same work on a reduced scale."

Before putting the cuttings in the cutting bed the amateur should run it a day or two in order to learn how to maintain an even heat.

HOW TO MAKE A CUTTING

All cuttings of the stems are made nearly alike, the only difference being that with different kinds of plants the length of the cuttings varies in proportion to the diameter of the stem and the distance between the buds. For instance: a geranium cutting is usually made about three or three and one half inches long, while that of a heliotrope is usually one and a quarter to one and a half inches long.

A sharp knife is needed so as not to bruise the stem. To make a good geranium cutting select a well-ripened end of a stem, cut it off at the required length, and just below a node (where a leaf is attached). It is important that the cut should be made just below a node, for roots are more freely produced than when the cut is made between the nodes. In many instances cuttings will not root at all if the cut is made anywhere but directly under the node.

Trim off carefully all the leaves except one at the top and trim off also all the stipules, those leafy growths on the stems where the leaves join. If these are left on they will decay and may lead to the cutting rotting, too.

Put the cutting in the sand, setting it deep enough to hold it erect, which will be

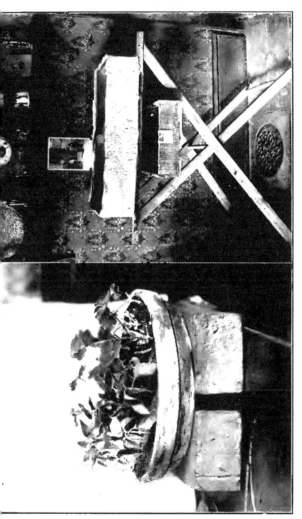

HOME PROPAGATION

On the right hand is an arrangement showing how the heat from the furnace is utilized in starting early seeds. The other picture shows a propagating pan on the kitchen range, the pan being stood upon bricks. Geraniums, salvias, coleus, etc., were grown here from cuttings

PROPAGATING GERANIUMS AND DRACENA

Geraniums are grown from cuttings which are merely taken off and inserted in the soil.
Dracenas sprout from pieces of the stem which are treated as seeds. See Chapter V

about three-quarters of an inch. If you are making a lot of cuttings quite a number can be made before putting them in the sand; but do not let the cut surface be exposed to the air too long or the chances of rooting will be greatly lessened.

Geranium cuttings should be set about an inch apart in the row, and the rows about two inches apart. If they are put closer they are much more likely to rot. Always dibble in the cuttings; simply forcing them down into the sand will injure the ends so that the cuttings will not root. After putting the cuttings in the sand, water them and shade them from the sun with a single sheet of newspaper. Other plants which may be propagated this way are heliotrope, ageratum, coleus, abutilon, hydrangea, etc.

The dracæna is another plant which may be cultivated by cuttings of the stems, but instead of making these cuttings as I have described for the geranium, the long, bare stem is cut into pieces two or three inches long, each of which must have a node, and the pieces laid down in the sand — they should be just covered. Each piece will make at least one new plant. When the new growth is $2\frac{1}{2}$ to 3 inches long, it is taken off the old stem and put in the cutting bench just like any cutting of the stem. The old stem is left in the sand for it frequently will provide more cuttings.

The bouvardia (one of the best plants one can grow for cut flowers at Christmas time) is increased in much the same way, but instead of cutting the stem into small pieces the root is cut up and the pieces treated exactly as if they were seeds.

PROPAGATING BY LEAVES

That new plants can be made from the leaves of old plants is a never failing source of interest to a great many people. The plant which is most commonly propagated this way is *Begonia Rex*. Take an old leaf and turn it upside down on a board, and with a sharp knife cut the veins. Then place the leaf right side up on damp sand, pin it down with toothpicks which have been bent in two, and shade it. At each cut in the leaf's vein a new plant will be formed. As soon as they have made a couple of small leaves separate the young plants from the old leaf and pot them off in a sandy soil with lots of leafmould in it.

The pretty little marble-leaved peperomia is another plant propagated from the leaf, but instead of cutting the leaf it is laid on the sand and the leaf stalk covered up. The gloxinia may also be propagated by tubers forming at the cuts.

The umbrella plant (*Cyperus alternifolius*) is perhaps the easiest of all plants to propagate by rooting the leaves. It is the simplest anyway. Cut off the bunch of leaves with, perhaps, one-quarter or one-eighth of an inch of stem, and put it in water. Never allow the water to become stale, which is best done by adding to it a few pieces of charcoal. In a few weeks a new plant will be seen pushing up from among the leaflets. Carefully separate it from the old leaf and pot it up.

PROPAGATING BY OFFSET

Some plants produce a lot of suckers or rosettes at the base of the plant, near the ground. Familiar examples of this are hen and chickens, and the screw pine (*Pandanus Veitchii*). The former forms little rosettes which simply have to be taken off and put in sand for a short time. The suckers from the screw pine are taken off, the leaves shortened back to reduce transpiration, and then put in the sand like cuttings of other plants. They root in a few weeks.

PROPAGATING BY RUNNERS

Runners differ from offsets in that the plant produces a small wiry stem which will form a new plant if the end is covered with soil. The two commonest house plants increased by this method are the strawberry geranium and the sword fern. The strawberry geranium will form new leaves on these runners before roots are produced, so if there is not a chance to allow them to root in the pot before separating the young plantlets from the mother plant they may be taken off and put in sand like any ordinary cutting. The young ferns must be rooted before being separated from the parent plants.

MAKING NEW RUBBER PLANTS

A well-kept rubber plant will in a couple of years become too ungainly for the house. Many times one does not care to part with it because of some sentiment attached to it. Two things may be done to make a shapely plant. The quickest way to reduce the plant is to cut it down to within a foot or fifteen inches of the ground. New shoots will appear in a short time that will transform the stub into a shapely, round-headed tree.

The other thing to do is to make a slanting cut in the stem far enough from the top so that when cut off it will make a shapely plant. Put a small piece of wood or charcoal in the cut to keep it open. Over the cut lay some damp sphagnum moss, and be sure that it always is damp, but do not let it become too damp or it may get sour. In a few weeks new roots will be seen protruding through the moss. When a mass of roots has been produced cut the stem off below the moss and pot the plant, moss and all, in a good potting soil. Put it in a shaded place for a few days until the roots have taken hold of the soil.

This method is often varied by carefully splitting a pot in halves, putting them about the stem of the plant, and then filling the pot with a mixture of soil and sphagnum moss. The moss is added to prevent rapid drying out of the soil.

Any plant which will grow from cuttings may be increased by this method, but it is usually employed only on hardwooded plants like the rubber plant, ardisia, dracena, etc.

CHAPTER VI

IN SICKNESS AND IN HEALTH

The relationship between plants and people — High temperatures — Cold draughts — Bad watering — Dust — Chills — Unnecessary fussing — Coal and illuminating gases — Insect pests and remedies — Freak remedies.

THE ideal conditions for house plants are practically the same as for human beings; that is, a temperature of about 65 to 70 degrees during the day time, and 50 degrees to 55 degrees at night. It may not always be possible to maintain this warmth at night, but strive to keep as near it as possible.

Plants grown in a window will invariably turn to the light, and unless the position is frequently changed, they will become one-sided. To avoid this, turn the plants half-way around each day, so that each half of the plant will get an equal amount of light.

During the winter have a care that none of the leaves of the plants touch the glass during the night or when there is frost out-side, because it will at least chill, and maybe kill them.

On very cold nights move the boxes or pots away from the window and put news-papers in front of the glass, but leave a dead air space between.

The next consideration is fresh air; keep the rooms well ventilated, *i. e.*, have a win-dow open somewhere in the room, preferably on the opposite side from the plants, for they cannot stand draughts. When a room gets too warm and too dry, the plants trans-pire an excessive amount of water — faster than the roots can supply it from the soil — but, worse still, the surface of the soil itself is dried out, and even the pot as well. Thus an irreparable injury is done before the owner realizes it.

TOO HIGH A TEMPERATURE

When plants are grown in an abnormally high temperature, with moisture, the growth is forced, and, being soft, is easily injured. A strong draught, even if only 10 degrees or 20 degrees cooler than the surrounding air, will seriously chill plants in this condition. The result will be that plants like the geranium and heliotrope will turn yellow and drop their leaves; with palms, the tips of the leaves will turn brown. To get the plants back into proper condition will take months of careful attention, and in the case of palms or ferns it will take a year — preferably at the florist's.

To give the atmosphere the proper amount of moisture have a small dish on the radiator, register, or stove, and keep it full of water. Most hot air furnaces have a water compartment inside the jacket which holds about a pailful. Under ordinary conditions this will need filling only once a day, but during the coldest days of winter, when the firing is heavy, it may be necessary to fill it twice.

WATERING

The second most exacting requirement of plants is watering. Too much water will make the soil sour; with too little water the plant will wilt. The effect of either will be yellowing and dropping of the leaves. It is easier, however, to drown a plant than to kill it by drought. No hard and fast rule for watering can be made. Plants may need water twice a day or only once in two days. The best way to determine whether a plant is dry is to rap the pot sharply with the knuckles of the hand. A hollow, or ringing sound shows that the soil needs water; a heavy, dull sound indicates that it has sufficient moisture. Usually you can tell whether the soil needs watering by looking at the surface. If it is dry and powdery give water.

The common fault in watering is not doing the job thoroughly. Never give a little surface sprinkling. The best way, if convenient, is to take the plants to the sink or bath tub and give the soil a good watering, allowing the pot to stay in the sink until the surplus water has had a chance to drain off. If it is impossible to do this, have a saucer under each pot and ten or fifteen minutes after the watering go around and turn out all the water standing in the saucers. Never allow water to remain in the saucers as it will prevent aëration through the hole in the bottom of the pot, and also it will rot the roots. When plants are kept in jardinières people often grow careless, let water collect in the bottom and then wonder why the plant is not doing well.

If by any chance the ball of earth should become very dry, plunge it in a pailful of water and let it stand five or ten minutes — until the whole ball is soaked through. When the air-bubbles cease to rise the ball is generally thoroughly soaked. Pouring water on the top of the soil of a dried-out pot plant is generally useless because the ball contracts in drying and leaves a small space between itself and the pot down which the water will run.

DUST ON THE LEAVES

Bathe the leaves frequently to remove dust, which will inevitably settle on them and choke up the pores. When the plant is in the sink or tub a hand syringe can be used to spray the foliage without wetting the floor. If this is inconvenient then carefully rub over the surface of each leaf with a damp sponge. If necessary, a little soap may be used in the water.

DISTURBING THE ROOT

Many amateurs do serious injury to their house plants by not leaving well enough alone while growth is dormant, or almost so. It is simply folly to fuss about with potted plants at that season. Do not disturb the roots at all during the winter, for most plants are resting and cannot quickly put out new roots. This is particularly true of such decorative plants as palms, rubber plants, and ferns, which can be shifted or fed with fertilizers only in summer. Soft wooded plants, like geraniums and heliotropes, are not so easily injured by transplanting, but even so I prefer to put them in large enough pots in the fall so that they will not need shifting until spring. If they should need extra feeding, on account of large growth, it is much better given in liquid form.

LIQUID FERTILIZERS

The best form of liquid plant food is made from cow manure — at the rate of two bushels to a barrel (fifty gallons) of water — because there is no danger of burning the roots; horse manure and sheep manure are also good, but they must be used very weak (one bushel of the former, and one-half bushel of the latter to a barrel of water) or they will injure the roots. I have used horse manure very successfully when the liquid was the colour of very weak tea. These are mussy to handle. Neater are the special plant foods put up in tablet, liquid, or powder forms. These can be bought in the local stores, or ordered from the catalogues of seedsmen.

If you wish to make a good liquid fertilizer at home the following recipe will give satisfaction. To one gallon of water add eight ounces of nitrate of soda, sixteen ounces of monobasic calcium phosphate, and ten ounces of sulphate of potash. For use dilute it, using one part of this stock solution to thirty parts of water, and use it about once a week.

COAL OR FURNACE GAS

Perhaps the greatest enemy of plants grown in houses heated by hot air furnaces or coal stoves is coal gas. An otherwise imperceptible trace of it in the air will cause the leaves of some plants (as Jerusalem cherry) to drop off promptly. With a good chimney draught and with proper regulation of the dampers when attending to the fire there should be no trouble from this source.

Illuminating gas is almost as bad as coal gas. The slightest trace will retard the development of new leaves on all but the toughest-textured plants, like rubbers and palms. Such thin-leaved plants as geranium, coleus, heliotrope, and begonia succumb quickly. When gas is present in very small quantity the plants do not necessarily die but growth is stunted and the flower buds wither when beginning to show colour, looking much as though they had been chilled.

TOBACCO FOR PLANT LICE

The commonest insect enemies of house plants are the plant lice or aphides. Look for these pests on the under side of the leaves where they suck the sap. Against them use tobacco water or soap suds. Tobacco water can be made from tobacco "stems" which can be bought from almost any florist or seedsman. Put a large handful into a gallon of warm water and let it stand for twenty-four hours, then dilute it to the colour of weak tea and syringe the foliage, being careful to hit the under side of the leaves. A simpler way is to buy a tobacco extract and follow the directions on the package.

If soap suds are used rinse the plants with clear water afterward.

If the plants are grown in a conservatory, or a room that can be completely shut off from the rest of the house, fumigating is the easiest and best method of fighting the aphides.

For this tobacco stems can be used, but the tobacco preparations offered in the stores are easier to handle, according to directions.

One can now buy sheets of paper which are impregnated with tobacco, and all that is necessary is to distribute enough sheets about the room to give the required density of smoke and set them afire.

Whatever method is used select a quiet night for it and shut the room tight. By morning all evidences of the smoke will have disappeared. Then syringe the plants to knock off the aphides. Badly infested plants will need fumigating twice a week on successive nights.

A SIMPLE FUMIGATOR

A simple fumigating device may be made from a soap box and three or four paper flour sacks. Turn the box upside down and in the bottom bore a lot of one-inch holes. In one end of the box make a hole big enough to put a saucer through. Cut open the sides of the bags in such a way that they can be pasted together again to make one large bag, the open end of which will fit over the box.

Now place the plant or plants to be fumigated on the still inverted box and draw the big paper bag down over them and tie it securely to the box with a string. In the saucer place one of the forms of tobacco — ground tobacco, or tobacco soaked paper or tobacco punk — light and place it inside of the box. Be very careful when fumigating the plants not to use the tobacco too strong or the leaves will become scorched. When the sack has become sufficiently filled with tobacco, remove the burning tobacco from the box. Let the plant stand half an hour with the sack on, then remove it, and syringe the plant with water to knock off the stupified aphides. Two light fumigations on succeeding days is much less liable to injure the plant than is one strong fumigation.

THE ROOT APHIS

An aphis sometimes attacks the roots, causing the plants to take on a sickly or

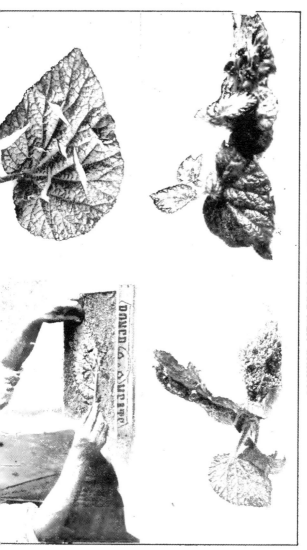

MAKING NEW BEGONIAS FROM A LEAF

A single leaf of the Rex begonia is cut through the veins and laid down on some light soil. New plants develop where the veins are cut

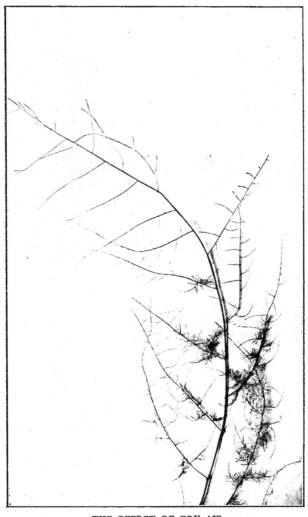

THE EFFECT OF DRY AIR

One of the commonest causes of trouble with house plants is an undue dryness of the air, causing the young growing tips of the plants to collapse and die. Illuminating gas in small quantities is equally fatal

yellow colour. It is easily found by digging down near the base of the stem, and is attacked by watering with the tobacco water already described. If this does not kill the aphides the plant must be removed from the soil, the roots washed with whale-oil soap (one quarter pound to two gallons of water). Then rinse and repot in fresh, clean soil.

RED SPIDER

Next to the aphides in destructiveness is the red spider, a very small red mite which can scarcely be seen by the naked eye. It lives on the under side of the leaves, but its presence can be readily told by numerous minute yellow spots on the upper side. Like the aphis the red spider subsists on the plant's juices. It thrives in a hot, dry atmosphere, and its presence is a sure sign of insufficient moisture. The conditions ordinarily found in living rooms are very favourable for this pest. The remedy is obvious: syringe the plants with water, applying it on the under side of the leaves, and with considerable force because the spider is protected behind a web.

Mealy bug, which is almost always present in the greenhouse, sometimes infests house plants, too. This insect looks like a small tuft of white cotton, and is found on the under side of the leaves and in the joints. A strong stream of water will usually wash it off, but if that fails use kerosene emulsion or fir tree oil, which must be diluted according to the directions on the package, and applied as a spray or with a feather. Alcohol has also been successfully used when there were only a few mealy bugs. With a feather or small stick put one drop on each bug, and he will immediately succumb.

VARIOUS SCALES

Very often scale insects will be found on the leaves of palms, ferns, rubber plants and cycads. The commonest one is the brown scale. It is one-quarter to three-eighths of an inch long, and nearly as wide, and its hard, convexed shell is dark brown in colour. The other scale commonly found on greenhouse plants is white, and about the size of the head of a pin.

Both these scales can be removed easily by spraying with whale oil soap, kerosene emulsion, or fir tree oil.

THRIPS

Sometimes plants are infected with thrips, which eat the epidermis of the leaves. They are small, slender, brown or black insects, about one-fourth of an inch long, and are easily controlled by any of the contact insecticides already mentioned, or by Paris green — one teaspoonful to twelve quarts of water.

If angleworms infest the soil in the pots they may easily be got rid of by watering with lime water which may be made as follows: To ten or twelve quarts of water add one and one-half to two pounds of fresh lump lime, letting it stand for a couple of days, or until the lime has slacked and the water cleared, then pour off the clear water for use. Several waterings with this at intervals of three or four days will drive out the worms.

FREAK REMEDIES

There are numerous freak remedies sometimes suggested for ailing plants, varying from applying beefsteak and castor oil to the roots, to coating the leaves of such plants as rubber trees and palms with milk or olive oil.

I never could understand why plants should need castor oil; in fact, it is a decided detriment, for it will clog the soil. When the plant begins to look sickly, look at once for the conditions which have caused it; it may be one of the causes mentioned in this chapter. There is a popular fallacy that if iron filings are put in the soil in which sickly plants are growing, their youth will be renewed. There is sufficient iron in any soil for plants, and any addition to the soil will be only a waste of time and money.

I can readily understand why wiping off the leaves with milk or other oily substance is resorted to; it makes the surfaces of the leaves shine. Every time this is done it is at the expense of the plant's health, for the fatty substance will surely clog the pores of the leaves, retarding or completely stopping the transpiration. The leaf of a healthy rubber plant or palm will shine if the dust is wiped off each day. This should always be part of the daily routine in the care of house plants.

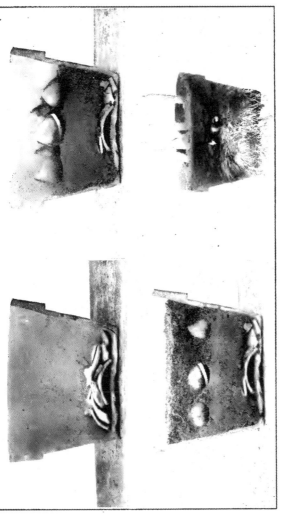

HOW TO POT BULBS

First give plenty of drainage. Half fill the pot with soil and put the bulb in position. After adding more soil, bury the pot in a cool place, so that roots may develop. Bring into light and heat, and begin forcing when the growths have attained the size shown in the last picture. Failure to flower results from forcing before roots develop properly

FORCING BULBS IN THE HOUSE

The crocus is generally regarded as one of the most unsatisfactory bulbs to force, but it will respond if not hurried too much. The upper view shows the stage when the pots are brought into the light. Note the excellent foliage

CHAPTER VII

Bulbs from Thanksgiving to Easter

The Dutch and Cape groups — How they differ — Tulips, hyacinths, and daffodils — Potting and rooting — Bringing into the light — Time required — Oxalis, fuchsias, sparaxis, and ranunculus.

THE easiest plants for the amateur to grow in the window garden are the bulbs. Roman hyacinths can be had by Thanksgiving; indeed, it is hard to fail with these charming flowers, and they come in red, blue, and white.

There is a long list of available bulbs, but most of them belong to one of two classes — Dutch bulbs and Cape bulbs — and all of each class used need similar treatment.

THE "DUTCH" GROUP

The bulbs which are known as "Dutch" in the trade are tulips, hyacinths, narcissus, crocuses, snowdrops, etc. To these might be added the Bermuda and Madonna lilies, because they require much the same treatment.

When the bulbs are received from the bulb merchant, about October 1st, put them in a good soil. I have used the soil described in Chapter II. Leafmould is not an essential, but I prefer to use it.

Put the bulbs in pans rather than in pots. Six-inch pans are the best for the small bulbs like crocuses, snowdrops, and bulbocodiums; the polyanthus narcissus are generally grown in six-inch pots; one, two, or three bulbs to a pot, according to the size of the bulbs. Tulips, hyacinths, and daffodils are best grown in eight-inch pans. Pans look better than pots — there is not such an expanse of red clay — and besides, they do not take up as much room. Set the bulbs to a depth to have them just covered with soil. After potting give them a good watering and set them away to make roots.

The secret of bulb culture lies almost entirely in the root development. If the bulbs are not well rooted before they are forced they will not make good flowers.

But no amount of care will increase the

number of flowers, for that is already determined — the buds are already formed in the bulb — but the size of the flowers depends largely upon having good heavy bulbs and giving them proper treatment before forcing. To secure a good root system on the Dutch bulbs put them, after potting, in a cool, dark place and keep the soil moderately damp for at least six weeks, except that Roman hyacinths can be forced after three weeks, and will flower in two or three weeks. I prefer to bury the bulbs about a foot in soil outdoors. When the ground begins to freeze a mulch of leaves or manure, sufficiently thick to keep the soil from freezing, is put on them. Here they are left until wanted for forcing.

One amateur solved the winter storage of her bulbs as follows:

"The construction of the pit was of the simplest. A bottomless box was sunk in the ground to a depth of three or four inches — enough to make it stand firm. This left an enclosing board frame about nine inches high above the ground level. Inside this frame the earth was dug out to a depth of eighteen inches, and a layer of coarse coal ashes spread on the bottom, to insure good drainage. On this foundation the pots of bulbs were placed. The spaces between the pots were filled with sphagnum, and a layer of moss was laid over them. The box was then filled in with clean oat straw, tucked in with a warm blanket of old carpet, and instead of a glass sash a tight wooden lid was fitted on and held in place by pine boughs. All these precautions are necessary here, for the thermometer sometimes registers 35 degrees below zero!"

ROOTING IN THE CELLAR

If neither of these methods is convenient, and you have a *cool* cellar, put the pots in a dark, out of the way corner and cover them with a foot or so of soil. Here they will always be handy for bringing into light and heat as required; but watch out that the mice and rats do not get at them.

For Christmas flowers force Paper White and polyanthus narcissus, Roman hyacinths, and the Duc van Thol tulips. They will require four weeks (except for the hyacinths, which are one week less) after being brought out into the light. The other Dutch bulbs will not force well so early in the year, and should not be brought into heat until about Christmas time, or later, according to when the flowers are wanted.

By bringing in the pots in batches in succession, at intervals of say ten days apart, flowers can be had from about January 20th until outdoor spring flowers appear. The pots or pans merely need digging from the ground and being put in the window garden, and the bulbs will at once commence to grow if not exposed to frost. On very cold or windy nights move them back from the window. They cannot help flowering if given decent treatment. Failures with bulbs are due, largely, to careless treatment.

THE BEST TULIPS

Good tulips for early forcing are Proserpine, Yellow Prince, Chrysolora, Vermilion Brilliant, La Reine, Rose Grisdelin, Cottage Maid. The other varieties do better if not started until late in January or early February. Do not try to force double tulips until late in February.

To get the Easter lily in flower for Easter, forcing must be started early — not later than December 1st — varying the heat according to the progress made. The lilies are grown one to a six-inch pot or several to an eight-inch pot.

The easiest bulbs to grow are the Roman hyacinths which may even be had in flower at Thanksgiving, Chinese sacred lily, and Paper White narcissus. These can be grown in water, or in cocoanut fibre or sand, requiring the same treatment as in soil.

The easiest plant to grow in pure water is the Chinese sacred lily; but you must be careful not to let a cold draught strike the buds or they will "blast." Heat causes the same thing. A temperature of about 50 degrees at night will give the best results. Get a shallow bowl and put in enough prettily coloured pebbles to hold the bulb in position.

To grow hyacinths in glasses select only the named single varieties that are specially recommended for this purpose. Use soft rain water. Put in a few bits of charcoal. See that the base of the bulb is always in contact with the water and don't let the water rise much above the base of the bulb. Keep the glasses in a cool, dark, well ventilated place until the roots reach the bottom of the glass. Then bring them into light and warmth. Don't put them near a gas jet, especially one that leaks. Move them away from the windows on cold nights. Change the water every few days. The patent glasses make this operation easier. Add two or three drops of ammonia once a week to the water.

THE "CAPE" GROUP

The Cape bulbs consist of such bulbs as freesia, ixia, sparaxis, oxalis — bulbs from the vicinity of the Cape of Good Hope.

As the bulbs are small I believe the amateur should plant them in five-inch pots. He can then make a few bulbs last over a greater season by bringing a pot at a time into heat at intervals of ten days. By starting the freesias and oxalis in August they can be had in flower at Christmas; the balance of the bulbs will do much better if not forced until after Christmas.

The Cape bulbs cannot be stored away in a dark place; they must have a light, cool, but frost-proof place in which to start growth, because they make some leaf growth as the roots develop. A cool room, having a temperature of 35 degrees to 40 degrees at night, and not higher than 50 degrees during the day, will be excellent. From here they can be brought into the window of the living room as wanted.

The ease with which the oxalis and freesias can be grown, and their beauty, are certainly attractions enough to induce anyone who has inclination to grow flowers to try them in the window.

The ixia and sparaxis, however, are seldom met with even at the florists. Both are cool-loving plants. The ixia does best when grown in a night temperature of 35 degrees or 40 degrees, with a rise of 10 degrees or 15 degrees during the day. It sends up long, grass-like leaves, and finally a long flower stalk, sometimes eighteen inches high, which ends in a spike three to eight inches long, of red, white, or blue flowers, according to the variety. The spikes contain six to twelve flowers, each of which is anywhere from one to two inches in diameter. If successfully flowered they are worth all the time and trouble you have gone to to produce them.

The sparaxis is much less known than the ixia; in fact, some bulb merchants never catalogue it, yet the European dealers recognize as many as twenty-five distinct named varieties. The plants grow six to twelve inches high, and each one produces from one to three or four flowers, each of which is one to two inches across, and funnel-shaped. It can be grown in the temperature of the ordinary window garden with success, for in the greenhouse it succeeds admirably in a temperature of 55 degrees at night.

If you have a cool corner in your conservatory or a window in a cool room, grow some of the named varieties of the poppy-flowered anemone (*A. coronaria*) and the turbaned or Persian ranunculus (*R. Asiaticus*). They are excellent either as pot plants or as cut flowers. Give them the same treatment as the Cape bulbs, and you are sure to succeed.

The poppy-flowered anemone has a pretty, finely divided leaf and a flower anywhere from one and a half to two and a half inches across, red, white, or blue in colour, and with a big bunch of blue stamens. It grows six inches to a foot high. If you buy any of the tubers of these I 'll wager you will look at them twice. and then begin to berate the bulb merchant for selling you some old, dried-up tubers, because they are very small, peculiar-shaped things, which apparently have no top or bottom. I must confess I never know whether I have some of them right side up or not. And because of the ease with which a bulb merchant can deceive a customer who is not acquainted with these tubers. I am sorry to say that some unscrupulous dealers have sold two or three year old bulbs as fresh ones. Of course they did not grow. The temptation to do this is great because the sale for them in this country is small; so buy from some seedsman in whom you have confidence.

The ranunculus has a fleshy root which looks like a lot of dimunitive sweet potatoes, one-half an inch long, joined together at one end. the other end hanging free. The plants grow six inches to a foot high, and the flowers in the double varieties. which are the only ones worth growing. are ball-like, red or yellow, one to one and one-half inches across.

Here is a dollar collection of bulbs that gave one amateur flowers every day without a break from Christmas to Easter:

Chinese lilies, bloomed from December 23d to January 12th; Double Roman narcissus, bloomed from January 13th to January 25th; Grand Soleil d'Or narcissus, bloomed from January 22d to February 13th; Crocus, bloomed from February 7th to March 12th; Van Sion narcissus, bloomed from March 7th to March 25th; Princess Marianne tulip, bloomed from March 23d to April 9th.

How many bulbs to put in a six-inch pan is told in this list:

Crocus, six; Freesia, nine; Hyacinth, named, three; Hyacinth, miniature, five; Hyacinth, Roman, six; Ixia, six to nine; Narcissus, three to five; Oxalis, nine; Tulip, six.

Eight-inch pans are more effective for the large bulbs, and six-inch pans for the small ones. Try ten tulips, ten narcissi or eight hyacinths in an eight-inch pan. Many people like to grow hyacinths singly in five-inch hyacinth pots, which are an inch and a half deeper than ordinary flower pots.

CHANGE YOUR LIFE AT WWW.MICROCOSM.PUB

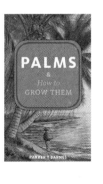

SUBSCRIBE!

For as little as $15/month, you can support
a small, independent publisher and get
every book that we publish—delivered to
your doorstep!

www.MICROCOSM.PUB/BFF